A BOOT UP

MINING WALKS IN CORNWALL & WEST DEVON

Peter Hancock

First published in Great Britain in 2011

Copyright © 2011 Peter Hancock

Front cover: *Wheal Coates near St Agnes from the Air* © Jason Hawkes
Back cover: *Pascoe's Shaft, South Wheal Francis near Camborne*

British Library Cataloguing-in-Publication Data
A CIP record for this title is available from the British Library

ISBN 978 0 85710 044 3

PiXZ Books
Halsgrove House, Ryelands Business Park,
Bagley Road, Wellington, Somerset TA21 9PZ
Tel: 01823 653777
Fax: 01823 216796
email: sales@halsgrove.com

An imprint of Halstar Ltd, part of the Halsgrove group of companies
Information on all Halsgrove titles is available at: www.halsgrove.com

Printed and bound in China by Toppan Leefung Printing Ltd

Contents

Introduction

During their heyday in the mid-nineteenth century the mining districts of Cornwall and West Devon were the world leaders in copper and tin production. Recognising this importance, in 2006 ten distinct areas of the region were jointly designated a World Heritage Site, providing the public with greater access. From major mines such as Devon Great Consols and the mines around Caradon Hill, to industrial complexes in Camborne, Redruth or the Luxulyan Valley, there is still much to appreciate.

The aim of this book is to highlight ten walks at a variety of different locations, from moorland settings to coastal paths, that provide an insight into our industrial past. At some sites engine houses and the remains of surface workings can be seen, elsewhere the focus is on transport links such as canals, tramways and railways. Whilst surviving remains often offer no more than a hint of the comprehensive structures that once existed above ground, they can still be evocative and atmospheric. Others, such as Wheal Coates or Wheal Trewavas, are blessed with spectacular natural scenery that overshadows man's brief intrusion, making the walk itself a special experience in its own right.

Care needs to be exercised near industrial remains, open leats, or when exploring exposed moorland or unfenced cliff paths. It is wise to remain on well-defined tracks near old mine workings, for open shafts can still be encountered; be extra vigilant if accompanied by children or dogs.

Where possible I have tried to make the walks circular. The distance provided for each one includes the return journey. Also, where they are available, alternative car parks are marked so the routes can be modified to suit individual requirements. For example, some can be shortened, while Walks 5 and 6 could be combined to provide a longer excursion.

The map references given are based on the Ordnance Survey Explorer Series which has a scale of 1:25 000, i.e. 4 cm to 1 km or 2.5 inches to 1 mile. As a wide range of walks have been included at diverse locations, a number of maps may be required. Having said that, it is hoped that once the starting points are located enough information is provided so that no other resources are necessary.

More information about most of the sites can be found in my companion book *The Mining Heritage of Cornwall and West Devon*, also published by Halsgrove.

The Luxulyan Valley: view across the remains of the china-stone mill.

Key to Symbols Used

Level of difficulty:

Easy

Moderate

More Challenging

Map symbols:

🚗   Park & start

     Tarred Road

– – –   Railway

– – –   Walk Footpath

     River, stream or brook

■   Building

+   Church

▲   Triangulation pillar or other landmark

👤   WC

🍽   Refreshments

🍺   Pub

Walk Locations

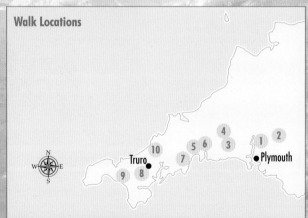

1 Devon Great Consols

Exploring major 'Consolidated' copper mines

For a long time inaccessible, the mines that formed Devon Great Consols have recently been opened up with a range of trails. This walk links six of these mines. However, it should be noted that little of the mid-nineteenth-century workings survive and most of what can be seen today dates from the period of arsenic production that followed the copper boom.

Level: 🥾 🥾 🥾
Length: 4.3 miles (7 km)
Terrain: Steep gradients in places; all on wide compacted stone paths.
Park & Start ref: Bedford Sawmills car park, signposted Tamar Trails, OS Map 108, 438726

Tamar Valley

Remains of the flues of the calciner used for recovering arsenic at Wheal Anna Maria.

7

In 1850 Devon Great Consols employed 1024 people, roughly half working underground and half at surface. At that time it was the largest and most profitable copper mine in Europe, with about 80 shareholders. Output reached a peak in 1856 when nearly 29 000 tons of ore were sold. However, significant mining and arsenic production had ceased by the end of 1901.

The view across the wooded Tamar Valley from Wheal Frementor. Some structures that were a part of the lower workings of Gunnislake Clitters Mine can just be glimpsed amongst the trees.

1 Bedford Sawmills was named after the Duke of Bedford, the land owner, and was part of Bedford United Mine. A branch line from here joined the railway to Morwellham. From the car park initially follow the Wheal Josiah Walk. Bear left at the marker post stating Devon Great Consols Railway Trail. From here the path drops downhill. Turn left following the yellow arrow for the Wheal Josiah Walk. The path passes Blanchdown Adit which drained some workings, the water stained orange by minerals. Then continue straight on at the marker post, heading for Frementor Mine. The path runs straight for a while then climbs steeply. Continue straight on at the hairpin bend. *(Alternatively, to shorten the walk by approximately a half and go directly to the arsenic works at Wheal Anna Maria and Wheal Josiah, turn right.)*

2 At Wheal Frementor in the southern part of the sett there is just a fenced shaft at the top of the rise. However the wonderful views across the Tamar Valley towards Gunnislake Clitters Mine make up for the lack of remains. Below here a leat from the river supplied a large waterwheel. This drove pumps via flat-rods that ran up the hillside to drain the Devon Great Consols mines.

Continue uphill through Blanchdown Wood. There is a fenced shaft on the left. The path then drops down into a valley.

3 Turn left for a short diversion to Wheal Maria. This mine was named after the wife of Josiah Hitchins who had gained the right to work the sett. Gard's Shaft, named after one of the shareholders, was responsible for the first significant

Despite the mine's significance, this stone archway is one of the few remains that can be seen at Wheal Maria.

Spoil heaps mark the site of Wheal Maria on the western side of Devon Great Consols.

A tranquil pond amongst the trees at Wheal Fanny is overlooked by a convenient picnic table.

copper ore bonanza, and at quite a shallow depth. Miners' cottages were built here as well as at Wheal Josiah. Today just spoil heaps remain, and a wall built as a settling lagoon.

4 Return up the slope to Wheal Fanny. This was named after Josiah Hitchins' daughter. Here ore was found just three fathoms beneath the surface. Further on is a pond — and picnic table. At the Wheal Fanny marker post turn right up a short steep path to Scrubtor. There is another welcome picnic table at the top! Turn

right at the marker for Wheal Josiah, then turn left down the hill.

5 Turning left at the junction, the 36 metre-tall arsenic stack at Wheal Josiah can be seen, as well as extensive sand-like spoil heaps from arsenic production. The conglomeration of surface buildings and equipment, including water wheels, are long gone.

6 Turn right down the slope at the granite marker post below the chimney for Wheal Anna Maria (Railway Trail). This mine was named after the Duchess of Bedford. A 40-inch pumping engine was moved here from another shaft in a record 14 days in July 1864 to augment the waterwheels during a very dry summer. In 1868 the arsenic works was constructed and

The chimney that served the arsenic flues, as well as ruined buildings at Wheal Josiah. Once a water wheel stood where the photograph was taken.

The crumbling remains of the arsenic works.

grew in importance as copper prices fell. Dressing floors, railway sidings, seven calciners, three refineries, as well as a laboratory, cooperage and warehouses where once here.

As well as a poison, arsenic was used to create green dye, popular on Victorian wallpaper – and even clothes. In 1888 alone Devon Great Consols produced some 2100 tons!

After the waste tips keep to the Wheal Anna Maria Railway Trail. The path snakes around huge spoil heaps. From here there are views of Gunnislake Clitters Mine and the tall stack at Greenhill Works forming a landmark on the far side of the valley. Look out for the partly-buried Wheal Josiah railway tunnel.

Initially ore was taken by carts to Morwellham, New Quay or Gawton Quay on the Tamar. Then in 1857 a railway was constructed to standard gauge from Wheal Anna Maria to a terminus above Morwellham 4.5 miles (7.2km) away. Two locomotives were used, as well as 60 ore and timber wagons at one point. For besides taking ore to the wharves, large quantities of Baltic and Canadian timber were brought up to the mines for shoring up the shafts.

The main workings of Wheal Josiah were up on the hill to the left, the pumps connected by flatrods that ran beneath the railway to the waterwheels in the valley. Also an inclined plane

The vast dumps of waste material scar the landscape, defying nature's attempts to reclaim them.

ran for 1260 feet (384 metres), taking ore down to the dressing floors. Here the path is fairly level as it follows the line of the track and runs through a cutting and over an embankment.

 Little evidence remains of Wheal Emma that once stood prominently at the top of the hill, its buildings housing a steam engine for pumping water, as well as a whim engine. This was the eastern extent of Devon Great Consols, opened in 1848, and named after the widow of the late William Morris who had been a

shareholder in the venture. By 1864 there were a staggering 42 miles of underground workings in the whole complex. Today just the fenced Railway Shaft on the left of the trail can be seen. The path now leaves the course of the railway and descends very steeply.

8 Turn left at the marker post, returning to the car park.

During its lifetime Devon Great Consols raised over £3.5 million worth of ore, the equivalent of about £218 million today!

2 **The Tavistock Canal**

Following the route of a forsaken form of freight

Following the accessible section of the Tavistock Canal from the busy town to tranquil countryside as far as the Lumburn aqueduct. Sadly it is not feasible to provide a circular route.

The canal, designed by John Taylor (1779–1863) was constructed in order to transport ore to Morwellham Quay on the River Tamar, while bringing

Level:
Length: 3.5 miles (5.6 km)
Terrain: Level footpath
Park & Start ref: Bedford Car Park, Tavistock, Map 108, 481743

coal and other materials up to the mines, as well as lime for the farms. It required a 2.4 km-long tunnel beneath Morwell Downs – no longer accessible – and an aqueduct over the River Lumburn, which will serve as the destination for this walk. Work commenced in 1803 and the complete canal was officially opened in 1817.

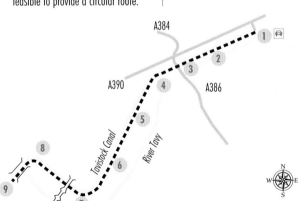

A384

A390

A386

Tavistock Canal

River Tavy

The Tavistock Canal emerges from beneath the old buildings of the wharf.

1. The car park was once occupied by coal and ore wharves at the head of the canal, as well as stables and warehouses. Returning briefly towards the main road, part of the canal can still be seen amongst the restored buildings.

2. Walk past Meadowlands Leisure Pool then follow the canal through 'The Meadows' park.

Running straight – and shallow – through the park. It was once five feet deep.

3 On the right a statue of Sir Francis Drake stands in the centre of the roundabout. However, from the park a pedestrian subway runs beneath the busy A386 to Plymouth. Now re-join the footpath beside the canal. On the right is the quaint row of Fitzford Cottages constructed in 1869. Tavistock College and its extensive grounds are on the left.

4 The canal takes a sweep left, leaving the growing suburbs behind. The sharp-eyed might notice a number of small quarries beside the canal along the route, and no doubt used during its construction.

5 The route passes close to Crowndale, the birthplace of Sir Francis Drake, the great Elizabethan

sailor and scourge of the Spanish. Wheal Crowndale was also once here; the original leat constructed to provide the copper mine with water directed from the River Tavy at Abbey Bridge in Tavistock formed the basis for the canal. In the early years of the nineteenth century it proved to be a very lucrative venture for John Taylor and the shareholders, with eighteen shafts sunk hereabouts.

The Tavistock Canal leading out of the town.

6 Soon it is possible to look down into the valley of the River Tavy, emphasising the unnatural route being followed by the canal. East Crebor copper mine was located here; in 1880 three miners drowned when the workings were flooded by the river.

The canal barges were about thirty feet long and of five foot beam, with a capacity of some eight tons. They were constructed of iron plate, probably in the foundries at Tavistock. A current of water helped move them downstream, but was a burden on the return journey.

The canal flows past tranquil woods and meadows, providing sustenance for cattle.

(7) The tow path veers to the right as it follows the contours of the Lumburn Valley. On the bend a small metal aqueduct takes the canal over a farm track from the valley below. Soon the tow path passes beneath the imposing viaduct, now sadly redundant. It once carried the South Devon Railway between Tavistock and Bere Alston which reached here in 1859 and, along with the decline in mining, led to the canal's demise in the 1870s.

Still waters reflect the trees and sky.

(8) The path soon reaches a lift bridge and lock gate, restored in 1998, fuelling the imagination with laden barges low in the water, sweating horses and their impatient handlers.

The lock gate and lift bridge, restored in 1998.

A view down the Lumburn Aqueduct, constructed in 1808 to carry the canal 60 feet above the valley floor.

(9) Around the bend an aqueduct takes the canal over the valley of the River Lumburn, some 60 feet (183 m) below, before abruptly terminating at a no entry sign. It is therefore necessary to re-trace one's steps. Anyway, a short distance further on it disappears into the tunnel. Here, in the 1850s, an attempt was made to use waterwheels to winch the barges through, but this system was abandoned, the men resorting to the laborious use of poles.

3 **The Caradon Mines**

Discover the great age of mining from boom to bust

Level: 🍂 🍂 🍂
Length: 4 miles (6.5 km)
Terrain: Footpaths, tracks and rough terrain, steep in places.
Park & Start ref: Minions. OS map 109, 260711, 262713, or 280697.

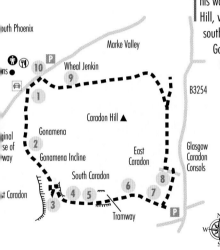

This walk takes a circuit of Caradon Hill, visiting the significant mines south of Minions via the Gonamena Incline and the Liskeard & Caradon Railway. The Caradon mines enjoyed a boom and bust existence; copper was discovered here in 1837, but by 1885 most had ceased operations. A walk around Caradon Hill provides an insight into what made this, for a time, the third largest producer of copper in Cornwall. From Minions it follows parts of the route of the Liskeard and Caradon Railway, as well as some tramways that served South Caradon Mine.

19

Today it is difficult to imagine the sleepy village of Minions at the heart of a major industrial complex, with railway tracks spreading out from it like the legs of a spider. In 1862 the line was re-laid, and a locomotive named Caradon replaced the horses. Subsequently, in 1864 and 1869 saddle-tank engines Cheesewring and Kilmar were purchased to serve the Liskeard and Caradon Railway.

(1) Near the Cheesewring Hotel, which declares itself the highest pub in Cornwall at 995 feet (303 metres) above sea level, is the start of a public footpath heading south along a lane. Pass through the gate and follow the path where many of the granite sleepers that supported the track remain in situ. Continue past the derelict cottage.

(2) Go through the farm gate. There is little to suggest that Gonamena Mine was once here. Ignore the farm track and bear right down Gonamena Incline, following the granite sleepers. The line was constructed during the 1840s. Look out for the

Above: The top of Gonamena Incline. West Caradon Mine is on the right, South Caradon on the left.

boundary marker stone carved with the initials LCR (Liskeard and Caradon Railway) at the top on the left-hand side.

Left: A boundary stone of Liskeard & Caradon Railway at the top of Gonamena Incline.

3 The large spoil heaps on the right-hand side of the path are the waste from West Caradon Mine. From here the railway continued southwards. Instead, turn left down the steep slope to the valley floor and cross the stream. This once powered waterwheels and was used to process the ore at what was South Caradon Mine. Within this valley there were tramways, cobbled dressing floors, as well as a conglomeration of buildings to cater for the needs of the mine and the miners.

4 Take the path up the eastern side. The ivy-clad engine house and chimney on the right mark Jope's Shaft, sunk in 1864 and later equipped with a man-engine to transport the miners to and from their labours. The path now follows the route of tramways which transported ore down to the dressing floors.

Jope's Shaft at South Caradon Mine, where a man-engine was installed during the 1870s.

5 The dramatic engine house at Rule's Shaft overshadows the arched entrance of the incline. Higher up the slope of the hill North Engine Shaft had its own tramway. Continue on towards the burrows. (Here two tracks run parallel but later converge.) Sadly little remains of the buildings that once stood above the tips at Kittow's Shaft which helped keep the mine profitable during the difficult early 1880s.

Approaching the engine house and tunnel entrance at Rule's Shaft, South Caradon. The path here follows the inclined tramway that took the ore to the dressing floors in the valley below.

6 From here follow the path as it bears right.

7 After passing beneath the telephone wires, turn left across the heath until meeting a gravel track leading to Wheal Tor Hotel, once the home of a mine captain.

8 Turn left towards the hotel, then right following the unmarked path between the burrows, all that remains of East Caradon Mine. On a fine day there is a magnificent view over east Cornwall towards Kit Hill and Dartmoor. The route of the railway, an extension built to overcome the impediment at Gonamena Incline, can now be seen ahead. On the right, across the road, a mine tip marks the site of Glasgow

The path veers right between the spoil tips that are all that remain of East Caradon Mine.

The northern course of the railway looks down on the sett of Marke Valley Mine and the village of Upton Cross.

Caradon Consols which operated from 1841 to 1885. Follow the left track which heads uphill. The right one was a branch line to Marke Valley Mine. The ivy-covered ruins of this enterprise can soon be seen as the track bears left around the northern slopes of Caradon Hill. Nestling in the valley close by is the village of Upton Cross.

(9) The two engine houses ahead were part of Wheal Jenkin. On the north-facing wall of the larger one at Bellingham's Shaft a plaque states M.V. 1886, for the sett was worked by Marke Valley at that time. It closed in 1890. Bear right across the embankment. On each side were once a range of surface workings, including dressing floors, ponds and leats.

(10) Turn left at the road which leads back to the car parks at Minions.

Left: The crumbling remains of the stamps engine house and stack at Wheal Jenkin near Minions.

Right: The robust and more recent pumping engine house at Bellingham's Shaft, Wheal Jenkin.

4 Following the Liskeard and Caradon Railway

Exploring an old railway and mine complex

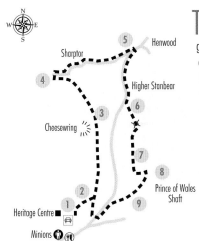

This walk is in two distinct parts. From Minions it starts gently following the route of the Liskeard and Caradon Railway as it passes below Cheesewring Quarry and heads north towards more remote granite quarries on Bodmin Moor.

The more challenging return leg drops down into the valley before visiting 'the well preserved buildings at the Prince of Wales Shaft of Phoenix United Mine.

Level: 🥾 🥾 🥾
Length: 3 miles (5 km)
Terrain: Varies. Level following the track, but also includes steep road sections and rough paths.
Park & Start ref: Minions. OS map 109, 263713

The eastern of the two car parks at Minions is the most convenient starting point. It also provides an opportunity to first visit the Heritage Centre at Houseman's

The view from the track towards Wheal Jenkin and Caradon Hill.

The Heritage Centre, occupying Houseman's Engine House.

Engine House. Constructed in 1881, it was part of South Phoenix Mine. Some time after the mine closed it was converted into a residence: notice the domestic chimney and altered bob wall. Despite any romantic notions they are not ideal for conversions, being rather cramped and dingy.

From here follow the path to the right of the buildings and down the slope in order to pick up the line of the track. Alternatively, if electing to miss the Heritage Centre, from the car park take the path just past the entrance to the road to Henwood and head north. Soon evidence of the track

Approaching Cheesewring Quarry.

will appear in the form of granite sleepers. The track ran through the sett of Phoenix United Mine. Once there were shafts on either side; now just a few remains of old buildings can be seen down the slope on the right.

 3 Follow the track beneath Cheesewring Quarry and past

Granite sleepers that retained the rails mark the path northwards. Cheesewring takes its name from the naturally weathered granite on the tor.

The granite quarries of Bodmin Moor were important in providing stone not only for the sleepers of the railway, but for mine buildings, London's Westminster and Tower Bridges, and other mid-Victorian building projects. The line was of standard gauge laid on granite sleepers at a time when the rest of the country's track was broad gauge on timber sleepers, while the wagons were initially propelled by gravity and horses. Later three tank engines were used, based at Moorswater near Liskeard.

large piles of discarded granite. Stowe's Hill is on the left. Continue until reaching the road. Here it was proposed to create a junction to provide an extension all the way to Trewint and Launceston. However this was never built, other than some preliminary earthworks.

Large amounts of granite were discarded to the south of the quarry.

Looking north towards Sharp Tor. As the track peters out our route turns right along the road.

(4) At the end of the fence turn right along the potholed road. (A short distance further on to the left the lane peters out and public access ends.) Continue down the hill and through the hamlet of Sharptor. There are spoil heaps on the right-hand side of the road, marking the northern extent of Phoenix United.

(5) At the crossroads turn right towards Minions. (Alternatively it is only a short diversion to the charming hamlet of Henwood nestling in the valley beneath Sharp Tor, once home to miners and quarrymen.) Follow the road up the hill through woods and past moss-covered moorstone. Looking back from here Sharp Tor dominates the landscape.

Sharp Tor dominates this part of the walk as the road climbs up from the valley.

6 At Higher Stanbear take the bridleway on the left. It drops steeply downhill and runs through the mine workings of Phoenix United. A wooden bridge crosses the stream. The steep climb on the other side leads past a jumble of moorland boulders and mine waste.

7 Turn left at the end of the spoil heaps. Marker posts with blue arrows provide directions past Phoenix House, a fine residence that was once the count house for the mine. On the left is the pond that provided water for the boilers of the steam engines.

The count house at the Prince of Wales Shaft is now a private residence.

When the other mines in the Caradon district closed in 1885, Phoenix United managed to continue by extracting tin. However, by 1898 even this was no longer viable. Ten years later a fresh effort began with a new shaft being sunk here on the eastern section of the sett, named after the Prince of Wales, the future George V.

Despite using up-to-date equipment, the new venture failed to extract sufficient ore or drain the mine effectively, and the outbreak of the First World War marked its final closure. This also signalled the end of the Liskeard and Caradon Railway.

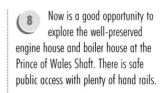

8 Now is a good opportunity to explore the well-preserved engine house and boiler house at the Prince of Wales Shaft. There is safe public access with plenty of hand rails.

9 Resume walking along the gravel track, once a branch line of the railway that served the mine, then follow the road back to Minions.

The engine house at the Prince of Wales Shaft, Phoenix United, with Cheesewring Quarry in the background.

5 Spit to Pont's Mill via the Par Canal

Explore the old route for cargoes of ore and stone

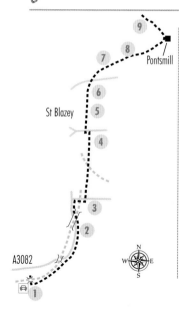

Level:
Length: 4 miles (5.6km)
Terrain: Mainly traffic-free and a level footpath.
Park & Start ref: Spit near Par. OS map 107, 074528

An easy walk that reveals a surprising amount of industrial archaeology mainly along level paths and away from the traffic. A car park is available at Spit on the A3082.

On the high ground behind the present-day clay dry was Par Consols; in 1849 it was the most profitable mine in Cornwall. During its heyday 15 pumping engines and whims were at work here, as well as steam-driven stamps and other processing equipment. An inclined plane was used to transport the ore to Par Harbour. However, the mine was unable to survive the copper slump of the 1860s. On the flat ground in the vicinity of the car park the smaller Wheal Par tin mine survived until the end of the nineteenth century.

A surviving section of the mineral tramway set in the path beside the canal.

① Take the path beneath the main Paddington to Penzance railway line, then immediately after turn left. Par Harbour and the large clay dries are presently owned by the French minerals company, Imerys. The harbour was constructed between 1829 and 1840, with a granite breakwater and wharves for the export of ore from Fowey Consols and its neighbours.

② Follow the pavement towards Par and beneath 'Five Arches' bridge. This is the least pleasant part of the walk. On the right was once Par Lead Smelting Works that required the landmark Par Stack, one of the tallest chimneys in the county, but demolished in 1907. It is difficult now to find this section of the canal that terminated at the harbour.

③ Turn right, and after the level crossing look for the first footpath on the left, keeping the river to your right. Granite sleepers in the path are remnants of an old mineral tramway. Take care crossing the railway track. Water now flows on both sides of the path.

④ At St Andrew's Road turn left over the level crossing, cross the road and resume following the footpath, signposted Rundle's Walk.

⑤ The path now passes close to St Blazey. The village expanded rapidly during the mid-nineteenth century. Looking to the left the square chimney stack of a group of old buildings is the Foundry and Engine Works, built by engineer William West in 1848, now a builders' merchants. St Blazey church can also be seen from the path.

Par Canal, almost hidden by vegetation.

Today's railway runs parallel to the old canal.

(6) On the right, at the foot of the hill, can be seen St Blazey Lime Kilns at what was Par Canal Wharf. This was removed when the canal was widened as part of the Par Flood Prevention Scheme. Note the one surviving side of the cast-iron

The old lime kilns, clearly modified over the years, form an impressive granite structure.

Canal Bridge. Take care crossing the busy road. Ahead, the tree line at the foot of the hill marks the edge of what was until medieval times the tidal limit.

(7) The tow path, deviating from the road, now grows more tranquil. It is a good place to spot wildlife, including the occasional heron.

The three-mile-long (5km) canal was constructed during the 1830s and incorporated three locks, the first one being tidal. Despite the locks being 90 feet long, no sign of them remains today. The horse-drawn barges were able to transport 52 tons of ore at a time from Fowey Consols. The site of this once highly profitable mine, one of the largest in Cornwall, is now marked by the ivy-covered Austen's Engine House on the skyline.

(8) Entering the wood at the foot of the hill, traces of industrial archaeology can be seen amongst the vegetation, as well as small sections of standard-gauge track and narrow-gauge tramway. The latter was laid between 1867 and 1870 to link two granite quarries to the canal, as well as carrying ore and mining supplies.

The canal and railway. Austen's Engine House can just be seen on the skyline from here.

Trevanney china clay dry is accessible to the public. The old ovens can be seen on the left, with the restored chimney stack framed by the doorway.

(9) The footpath joins a quiet metalled road leading to a car park. This forms the starting point for the next walk. Otherwise, a good termination of this walk is Trevanney china clay dry, a short way up the track. Go past the gate and ignore the footpath to the right. The track follows the Par River, containing amazing rounded granite boulders that look like a giant's discarded pebbles. The clay dry was used between the 1920s and 1960s, processing clay piped in from beyond the Luxulyan Valley. From here it is necessary to retrace one's steps, or continue on the next walk.

6 The Luxulyan Valley

Arboreal archaeology in a delightful setting

Sylvan tranquillity has replaced a busy industrial complex, leaving the constant sound of running water from a maze of rivers and leats.

These flowed to nearby mines, besides driving a waterwheel in the valley, a cheaper option than steam engines. An incline linked a tramway with the Par Canal.

Level: 🐾 🐾 🐾
Length: 2.7 miles (4.3 kms)
Terrain: Uneven paths, some level, others on a gradient. Muddy in places. Care needed near open leats.
Park & Start ref: Car park – OS Map 107, 074562 (or 058574).

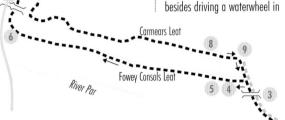

reffry aduct

Carmears Leat

Fowey Consols Leat

River Par

Carmears Incline

(1) The chosen start is the car park at Pont's Mill, just half a mile down a narrow lane from the A390, although there is another in the Luxulyan Valley itself. Follow the lane past the gate towards the valley. On the right a small hydro-electric plant harnesses the power of the streams flowing down the valley, and replaced a mill that once crushed china stone.

(2) Turn right past wooden posts to reach the foot of Carmears Incline. The granite sleepers that once supported the track remain in the path, and the eagle-eyed might spot the odd saddle or chair that secured the rails. To the left the former mineral railway has been absorbed into the railway network as the Par-Newquay Railway. Note the cambered sleepers

Carmears Incline.

The incline is 875 metres (½ mile) long and rises 100 metres (325 feet) from the canal. It was built in the 1830s at a cost of £3537.

on the bend in the incline. I have found no record of any derailment...

(3) The tramway that transported granite and china clay runs beneath an elegant granite. This which carries The Velvet Path — originally The Long Drive — once a private carriage drive built between 1840 and 1860 by Nicholas Kendall of Pelyn near Lostwithiel. After the bridge the incline runs through a cutting and then across another embankment.

The bridge over the incline carrying 'The Velvet Path'.

A view across the remains of the china-stone mill.

4 Turn left before the top of the incline, keeping the stream to the right. This, the Fowey Consols Leat, now combined with the Carmears Leat, supplied water to the mines on the neighbouring hill.

5 The growing roar of water is from the wheel pit. The waterwheel that was once here must have been a spectacular sight. Now only the hub remains.

6 After the bend the Luxulyan Valley opens out into pastureland. Then, beyond a large bolder straddling the leat, the vista is suddenly dominated by the Treffry Viaduct.

The wheel pit and surviving axle.

Surviving industrial archaeology, perhaps too heavy to remove for scrap.

The wheel pit was constructed during the 1840s originally designed to take a 50 foot over-shot water wheel, although initially a 30 foot one was employed. The wheel was used to raise the wagons on the incline using a cable. When this ceased in 1874 it was replaced with a 40 foot one to power china-stone grinding mills on either side. The stone bases of these buildings can still be seen, the top portions having been constructed of timber.

(7) Walk under the viaduct, still following the leat. A short distance further on turn right across the wooden bridge. (Another car park is just a little way ahead.) Follow the path up to the level of the viaduct and enjoy the views of the valley. Crossing the viaduct, the track soon becomes impassable. Instead it is better to go the other way, following the route of the old track, now with the leat initially to the left. A new boardwalk constructed by The Friends of Luxulyan Valley crosses a boggy patch. Small sections of track, granite sleepers, even the odd saddle, can be seen poking clear of the mud.

The viaduct was constructed between 1839 and 1842 under the instructions of Joseph Thomas Treffry who funded the £7000 project. It is 201 metres (660 feet) across and rises nearly 30 metres (100 feet) from the valley floor. Serving the local mines and quarries, the railway line continued to Newquay harbour, thereby linking both coasts. Besides taking the railway across the valley, beneath the track bed is an aqueduct: the water can just be seen through some of the larger joints. One can only marvel at its construction.

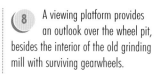 **8** A viewing platform provides an outlook over the wheel pit, besides the interior of the old grinding mill with surviving gearwheels.

9 Return down the incline, noting the various ruined buildings at the summit.

A surviving building marks the start of the descent down the incline.

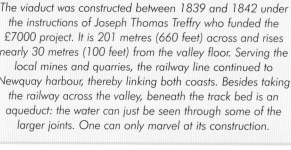

Left: The path, following the leat, runs beneath the Treffry Viaduct/Aqueduct.

7 Charlestown

An historic harbour community

Level: 💎
Length: 3.2 km (2 miles)
Terrain: Mainly minor roads and footpaths
Park & Start ref: Charlestown car park,
OS Map 105 or 107, 038517
Refreshments: There are various inns, cafes
and restaurants in the village.

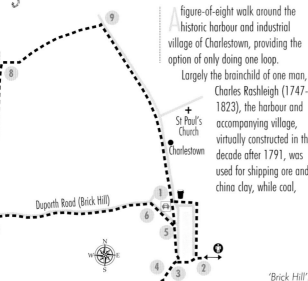

A figure-of-eight walk around the historic harbour and industrial village of Charlestown, providing the option of only doing one loop.

Largely the brainchild of one man, Charles Rashleigh (1747-1823), the harbour and accompanying village, virtually constructed in the decade after 1791, was used for shipping ore and china clay, while coal,

limestone and timber were brought in. Previously West Polmear or Porthmear before being renamed after its benefactor, it has changed little in over two centuries.

'Brick Hill'.

An empty dock. At one time it was filled to capacity with sailing vessels.

1 The car park was formerly a coal yard in which the imported fuel was stored, with a timber yard behind it. Cross to the left-hand side of the harbour. The Shipwreck and Heritage Centre occupies part of a former clay dry. Running beneath Quay Road, a tunnel was used to transport clay to chutes that fed it into the holds of waiting ships. This landward part of the harbour was once a boatyard and slipway. Over 30 vessels were constructed and launched here before the dock was extended in 1875.

The harbour master's residence is at the end of the pretty row of Regency cottages. A short distance up the coastal path one of the oldest buildings in the village, now called Salamander, was once the Content pilchard cellar where the fish was processed and barrelled: notice the holes in the wall where levers compressed the fish. (Further on are the only public conveniences in the village.)

2 Turn right down the slope and steps. The present harbour master's Round House was constructed in about 1900 on the site of a large limekiln, creating a dressing used by farmers to counteract the acidic Cornish soil.

Charlestown Harbour. An evocative scene, for it is now home to the 'Square Sail' fleet.

On the hill to the east was the very successful Crinnis Cliff Mine, active in the early years of the nineteenth century. By 1816 nearly 40 000 tons of copper had been carried by pack mule and shipped from the harbour. Once the shallow workings were exhausted levels were even driven out beneath the sea.

3 Cross the dock gates. These, lowering like a drawbridge, date from 1971 and replaced earlier wooden ones. Ahead, the Pier House Hotel, built in 1793, was first called the Charlestown Hotel, but has also served as a farmhouse.

4 It is worth taking a short diversion up the coastal footpath to the battery, also built in 1793, to protect the harbour from a possible French attack. On the right of the footpath the row of coastguard

The former Content pilchard cellar, now a private residence. Note the holes in the wall that were used during the processing.

cottages look out over the outer basin. Inside the crenellated battery walls are the gun platforms and the remains of a gunpowder magazine.

Charlestown Harbour, home of period tall-masted ships.

Return up the road on the western side of the harbour. The little cottage set back from the road was once an inn.

Charlestown Battery, built to defend the harbour.

5 Either return to the car park or continue on the longer loop of the walk by turning left into Barkhouse Lane. The shipwrights' workshops on the left were once pilchard cellars.

6 Follow Duporth Road to the left. It is still known locally as Brick Hill, for there was once a brickworks in the vicinity. Beyond the bank on the corner is the lower of two ponds, fed from Charlestown Leat flowing from the Luxulyan Valley (see Chapter 6) and used occasionally to flush out the harbour. (There is no access to it.)

The woods on the right are the site of South Polmear Mine. Now just a few spoil heaps can be seen beside the road, but as well as several shafts, dressing floors, a count house and gunpowder store, there was also a small quarry here.

On the left was the fine estate once owned by Charles Rashleigh. Sadly Duporth Manor was demolished in 1988, and the grand gardens are no more.

A view of the village from the battery, the rural setting disguising its industrial past.

7 At the top of the hill turn right, crossing the road to use the pavement. Across the fields a spoil heap can be seen; this valley was also mined, and there was once a whim (winding) shaft beside the road.

8 Look out for the footpath on the right. This runs through the grounds of Penrice School which encloses the Long Stone megalith on the left. There are fine views down the valley to St Austell Bay. There was once a mill and smelting works here. The path then emerges on to Charlestown Road. On the left amongst the trees was once a naphtha works.

9 Turn right to return down the hill. Charlestown Leat may be seen beside the road. This also supplied water to the surviving waterwheel – once one of four – amongst the new buildings on the left, the site of Charlestown Foundry. This business served the local mines, and later the china clay industry, before closing in 2003. The arched façade of the machine shop has been preserved in the modern apartments.

Opposite the entrance to Church Road is the old smithy. Also notice the Victorian post box. It is worth taking a short detour to visit St Paul's Church, completed in 1851, but not until the 1970s was the spire – of fibreglass – added. The next house in Charlestown Road was the home of the manager of Charlestown Estate.

The façade of the old machine shop of Charlestown Foundry has been incorporated in the new apartments.

From right to left; the old count house, lime kiln and gun store, all finding fresh contemporary roles.

The large granite building at the entrance of the lane once housed a stone-crushing plant. At the end of the cottages was a weighbridge. (Another survives near the car park.) Across the road the present park was one of a number of ore floors that occupied open spaces around the village. Further down the valley beyond the trees was a rope walk and several mineshafts. Continuing on the right-hand side, down a short

lane between the row of cottages can be seen the granary. The last two of the cottages set back from the road together comprised the farmhouse of West Polmear Farm. Then the old village school, constructed in 1895, can be seen down the next lane.

On the left-hand side of the road is the Methodist Chapel. The car park of the Rashleigh Arms was also an ore floor, its uneven surface cobbled with

ballast from in-bound ships. Meanwhile, the partly-timbered building on the right was once a count house, while the small residents' car park was a limestone floor that served the limekiln below. This has been turned in to commercial premises. Adjoining it is the gun shed where the weapons used in the battery were stored. Now turn right, back to the car park.

8 The Great Flat Lode

Exploring great cathedrals of industry

This circular walk visits some of the significant industrial remains to the south-west of Carn Brea. It was here during the 1870s that a rich lode of tin was discovered beneath copper lodes that had already been worked, and due to its relatively horizontal angle it was labelled the Great Flat Lode.

Level: 🐾 🐾
Length: 4.5 miles (7 km)
Terrain: Gentle gradients. Sound paths and minor roads – beware of traffic.
Park & Start ref: Marriot's Shaft, South Wheal Frances, OS Map 104, 681394.
Refreshments: The Brea Inn and The Countryman Inn, Piece.

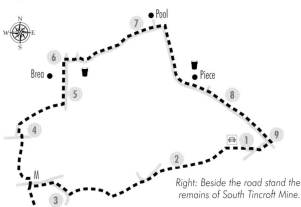

Right: Beside the road stand the remains of South Tincroft Mine.

① The walk begins at the main trail car park, close to the substantial buildings that survive at Marriot's Shaft, the South Wheal Frances section of Wheal Basset.

These impressive cathedrals to industry were at their zenith a century ago; a 40-inch and 80-inch compound engine was used here between 1899 and 1918, the only one of its type to operate in Cornwall. In 1896 a new company called Basset Mines Ltd united most of the mines working the Great Flat Lode, thereby creating a more efficient operation. A tramway once ran up to the buildings to transport the ore and bring in coal and other materials. As late as 1908, just ten years before the mine closed, the large miners' dry or changing room was constructed.

From here the path continues to the left of the sloping ore bin base.

Even in a roofless state, the buildings at Marriot's Shaft, South Wheal Francis, are still impressive.

On the left can be seen the miners' dry and changing room, just a short distance from the engine and boiler houses.

The commodious miners' dry and changing room, constructed in 1908.

Marriot's Shaft reached a depth of 310 fathoms (1860 feet or 567 metres), although it was planned to go down as much as 5000 feet (1524m). Originally crooked, it was straightened and made wide enough to accommodate an underground boiler and steam hoist, but the ambitious scheme failed to come to fruition. The shaft is now guarded by a large grille.

This well-built structure standing before the guarded shaft reflects the wealth and optimism that the Great Flat Lode engendered.

The path passes two engine houses at Pascoe's Shaft, South Wheal Frances. The first was built in 1887 and contained an 80-inch pumping engine, while the winding engine house was built in 1879 for a 30-inch beam engine. Follow the road to the left, then continue straight on down the bridleway as indicated by Great Flat Lode signs, past miners' cottages. At the gate turn right down the lane with a Mines marker post. Daubuz' Shaft engine house with its truncated stack, also part of South Wheal Frances, is on the right. This was built in 1880 and contained a 30-inch engine. On reaching the lane turn right, ignoring the Great Flat Lode sign.

 Ahead is Wheal Grenville, which can be reached via the stile. The two engine houses here at Fortescue's Shaft were constructed in 1892, the larger housing a 90-inch beam engine used to drain the mine, its companion a 28-inch winding engine. The mine closed in 1920. On the hill to the west is South Condurrow Mine. Both mines struggled to remove water, especially during the winter, and at a time when neighbouring mines had already closed.

The pumping engine house at Pascoe's Shaft, South Wheal Francis, erected in 1887, stands beside the path.

The two sturdy engine houses at Fortescue's Shaft, Wheal Grenville.

Continue following the road, bearing left at the junction. King Edward Mine Museum is soon on the right. Previously the training centre for

Woolf's Shaft pumping engine house was a late-comer in the history of the Great Flat Lode

Camborne School of Mines, it now provides an interesting insight into local mining and tin processing.

Just past the museum's entrance the Great Flat Lode Trail turns right into a bridleway. Alternatively take a detour up the path on the left to Marshall's Shaft of South Condurrow Mine. Four steam engines were once employed here; a 60 inch pumping engine, a 26 inch whim engine, as well as two operating stamps.

Bear left at the T-junction in the path (an engine house of King Edward Mine is on the right). The path now runs between fields. Bear right at the fork, following the main path.

4 Meeting the road, on the right is Great Condurrow Mine. Woolf's Shaft was probably named

after Arthur Woolf who developed the idea of compound engines (using more than one cylinder). This engine house is noteworthy for being built entirely of granite, and as late as the early twentieth century.

From the exit of the footpath turn left along Higher Condurrow Road, and after about 50 metres turn right into the lane following the Great Flat Lode signs. Continue to Carn Entral, then follow the bridleway to the right. At the top of the rise there are views on the left towards the north coast, with spoil heaps on the right. Dropping down the hill, a former count house, now a private residence, is on the left.

5 After exploring Wheal Grenville, continue following the road ignoring the Great Flat Lode signs.

Two large buddles used during the refining process at Brea Tin Streaming Works. On the horizon are surviving buildings around South Crofty.

Brea Tin Streaming Works is beside the road on the right-hand side. These were active during the 1890s. Here can be seen settling tanks and buddles used to separate out fine tin particles. This was one of 40 such refineries that took advantage of the Red River. Continue down the hill to Brea village.

6 Turn right immediately after Brea Methodist Chapel, then right again following the leats, used to convey water to the mines. Pass The Brea Inn, and continue following the road to South Tincroft Mine.

7 The engine house beside the road was built in about 1860 and housed a 26-inch beam engine to work Dunkin's Shaft. Close by is a roofless compressor house and stack, built in 1891, thirty years before the

Warning: This is a busy road at certain times, and only partly provided with a pavement or grass verges.

mine closed. At the junction take the Four Lanes road and follow Penhallick Road, continuing up Whitecross Hill to the mining village of Piece.

8 Just after Piece is Thomas's Shaft Pumping Engine House of West Basset Mine. Built in 1854, it is the oldest surviving engine house on the Great Flat Lode. It housed a 60-inch engine that stopped working in 1899. There was a fire here in April 1896, one of a series to bedevil Wheal Basset. Now little more than the bob wall survives. Continuing along the road, spoil heaps can be seen on the left towards Carn Brea.

9 At the junction turn right, returning to Marriot's Shaft and the car park.

9 **Wheal Prosper, Rinsey, to Porthleven**

Dramatic coastal mines offering superb views

This walk takes advantage of the South West Coast Path to visit the well preserved engine house of Wheal Prosper overlooking Rinsey Cove, as well as the breathtaking engine houses on the cliff edge at

Level: 🐾 🐾
Length: 8 miles (13 km)
Terrain: Coastal path, steep in places. Optional return along quiet minor road.
Park & Start ref: Rinsey car park, OS Map 102, 592272
Refreshments: There are various places at Porthleven.

Wheal Trewavas before continuing to the former mining harbour at Porthleven. The return can be the same way, or via a minor road a little way inland.

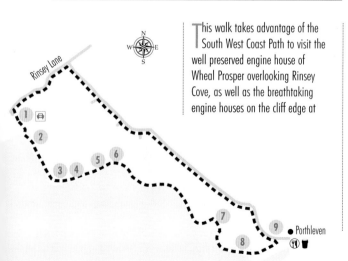

The solitary engine house of Wheal Prosper in a sublime setting overlooking Rinsey Cove.

(1) Walk down the path from the car park, or take a detour to the right down the path to the beach at Porthcew. (Although this would require a climb back up again.)

(2) The solitary engine house of Wheal Prosper only operated for five years following its construction in 1860. Despite its exposed location, it is in good repair, being in the care of the National Trust. From here the level path follows the sea.

(3) Spoil heaps that look like infertile orange sand are all that remains of the dressing floors on the approach to Wheal Trewavas. The path continues straight on, as directed by a marker post.

The bob wall faces the sea. The mine had a short working life.

(4) At Wheal Trewavas two engine houses are located part-way down the cliffs in a similar position to those at Crowns engine houses, Botallack. One can only marvel at the skill and bravery of the builders erecting these structures and installing the machinery in such a precarious and exposed position, as well as the surface workers who operated here. There is even a terraced platform built into the steep slope that held a capstan. As at Botallack, the shafts ran out beneath

A dramatic setting for the engine houses at Wheal Trewavas.

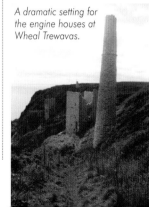

the sea bed. The flooding of these was the downfall of this mine. The site was given to the National Trust, and

Access has recently been improved, but care still needs to be taken. The precarious platform to the left of the engine house once supported a capstan.

the buildings were recently restored. A path now leads to the nearest engine house, but note the open shaft in front of the bob wall facing the sea.

5 After Trewavas look out for a spectacular outcrop of rock, balanced above a steep drop into the sea. Now the path zigzags down through bracken into a valley that looks like a natural amphitheatre.

6 It is a steep climb up the other side, then the path drops down to a cove at Tremearne Par. A little bridge crosses a stream, while steps lead down to the shore.

7 Here the path climbs up and around Parc Trammel Cove, hemmed in by sheer grey cliffs.

Looking back towards Wheal Trewavas from the coastal footpath.

8 The neat granite cross is a memorial to drowned mariners, as well as marking the passing of the 'Grylls Act' of 1808 that stated that bodies washed up by the sea should be laid to rest in the nearest consecrated ground. On the seaward side is a dedication to 22 Porthleven fishermen lost in a number of disasters at sea. It was erected in 1949.

The cross erected in memory of drowned mariners photographed overlooking a tranquil sea.

9 The footpath ends at the 'Wrestling Fields', perhaps a reference to Cornish wrestling being enjoyed here. The walk continues down the hill to the harbour. The original harbour was constructed during the early nineteenth century. Then in 1855 Harvey & Co. of Hayle acquired it to provide a fresh transport link to serve the local mines. They were responsible for constructing the breakwater and lock gates. Later china clay was also shipped from here.

The Burial of Drowned Persons Act, also known as the Grylls Act, was brought about following the loss of the Royal Naval frigate HMS Anson just along the coast the previous year. Witnessing the tragedy also inspired Henry Trengrouse to develop a rocket and breeches buoy to save wrecked mariners.

The return walk can be back along the coastal footpath, or just before The Wrestling Fields a minor road branches to the right where a sign on the wall reads Claremont Terrace, then following a fairly direct route and only a little way inland heads back to Rinsey Lane and the car park.

Looking across Porthleven outer harbour towards the distinctive Bickford-Smith Institute, built in 1883 on the site of an inn.

Porthleven Harbour once served the mines of west Cornwall.

Porthleven had its own mine, to the east above Porthleven Sands. Wheal Rose was active during the early years of the Industrial Revolution. It is recorded that it acquired a 58-inch steam engine from Wheal Liberty, St Agnes, in 1838. The church-like building with a clock tower at the harbour mouth is actually the Bickford-Smith Institute. It was built in 1883 as a scientific and literary institute, the £2000 construction cost met by William Bickford-Smith whose grandfather invented the miners' safety fuse.

10 Trevaunance Cove, St Agnes to Porthtowan

Mining heritage amongst the heather

Wheal Coates

P 7 • Chapel Porth

8

9 **P** • Porthtowan

This walk takes advantage of the South West Coast Path to visit a number of mines overlooking the Atlantic. A word of warning: it will probably not be enjoyed by walkers who suffer from vertigo, as the path is high above the sea with steep slopes down to the water.

One of the problems facing Cornish mines was transporting the hard-won ore to the smelters in South Wales. As mines surrounded Trevaunance Cove it was seen as a natural place to construct a harbour. However, despite five

Level: 🥾 🥾
Length: 9 miles (14km) including return.
Terrain: Coastal path of course sharp stones. Mainly level but steep in places.
Park & Start ref: OS Map 104 – Trevaunance Cove, 721516; or Porthtowan, 693482; Wheal Coates, 703500; or Chapel Porth, 697494.
Refreshments: A café mid-way at Chapel Porth, open during the summer, or Porthtowan.

attempts, all that remains of the endeavours are large granite blocks revealed at low tide. The harbour was never very substantial; an overhanging wooden stage was used to reach ships, while a chute facilitated the loading of ore. The final pier at this exposed location was lost to storms in 1915.

① Opposite the public conveniences near the beach some steps lead up to a path and tarmac road. Next to the beach once stood an old hammer mill, used for a time as part of a tin salvage works. It is easy to get romantic about our industrial past, but in the nineteenth century this whole valley would have been an unsightly complex of mine workings, rudimentary buildings and spoil heaps.

Pass through the gateway and ahead is a marker post for the footpath. But first look left to the large excavation that was Wheal Luna tin mine, with an impressive man-made stone arch high above some adits. Continue up the granite steps, noting the engine house at Wheal Kitty on the skyline.

② The chimney stack and spoil heaps on the left mark the sett of Polberro mine. It was known as Royal Polberro Consols after Queen Victoria paid a visit in 1846. A diversion inland leads to an engine house at Turnavore Shaft which last operated between 1937 and 1941. Further along the path conical mesh

Trevaunance Cove overshadowed by spoil heaps atop the cliffs.

Polberro Mine was equipped with steam-driven stamps that had 72 heads to strike the tinstone. Where favourable, water power was generally preferred.

The view back along the path towards St Agnes.

run parallel to each other for a short distance. The grey dome on the horizon is at the former chemical weapons establishment at Nancekuke.

(**4**) Crossing Tubby's Head the engine houses at Wheal Coates can be seen. St Agnes Beacon is on the left.

covers over open shafts may be seen on the right. Soon the path is crossing Newdowns Head, owned by the National Trust. Bowden Rocks or 'Man and his man' can be seen out at sea.

(**3**) Reaching the crest at St Agnes Head Coastguard Station the view ahead opens out, and two paths

Looking west towards Wheal Coates.

The sett of Wheal Coates has a dramatic location.

much-photographed Towanroath pumping engine house. It was constructed in 1872 and is now in the care of the National Trust.

(7) The path soon splits into a variety of routes of varying degrees of difficulty, all heading towards Chapel Porth. This small cove is a popular spot for surfers, and in the summer months a small café offers welcome refreshments. It is a steep climb out of Chapel Porth up a stony path.

(5) As the engine houses are approached the path branches left and right. Take the left path towards the higher workings. Furthest inland is the remains of the whim (winding) engine house, built in 1880. Behind it amongst the heather is a rectangular bank and wall marking the pond that supplied the boilers of the steam engines with water. The other engine house, used to power stamps and a whim, was built in 1872-3. The calciner which was used to produce arsenic from 1910 to 1913, its stack, as well as some flues, can also be seen.

(6) Follow the path down the slope to the lower coastal path. Here can be found one of the most evocative and atmospheric industrial remains in Cornwall, the

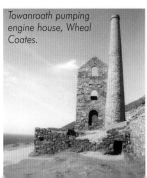

Towanroath pumping engine house, Wheal Coates.

Destination Porthtowan, and in the centre of the picture the engine house of still-born Wheal Lushington.

8 A short way on, and surrounded by infertile mounds of mining waste, stands the solitary remains of the bob wall of the pumping engine house at Wheal Charlotte. This copper mine suffered from its remote location — as can be seen — experiencing difficulties with transport.

9 Approaching Porthtowan, near the beach can be seen a converted engine house that was once Wheal Lushington. The building was completed in the 1880s, but the company went bankrupt before the engine was installed. From Porthtowan the walk can be extended up the valley where there are engine houses at Wheal Ellen (703469), Tywarnhaile Mine (700472) and United Hills (696475). Otherwise it is necessary to return the same way...

Conclusion

It is hoped that these walks will have proved enjoyable and informative. There are many other prescribed walks, particularly in the Camborne/Redruth area, such as the Coast to Coast Trail. Others are still being developed, namely in the Tamar Valley.

Or perhaps they will inspire some to seek out less well-trodden paths around what remains of our industrial past. This can be more challenging. It was hoped to include a walk encompassing the once important tin mines of Polgooth near St Austell. At its peak at the end of the eighteenth century some 1200 people were employed here, yet today little evidence of their activities remains, and the three surviving engine houses are all on private land. Similarly the once great Fowey Consols, for a time the largest copper mine east of Gwennap, has all but vanished. Surely the unsung men, women and children who laboured in our mines deserve some recognition for their contribution to our industrial legacy, leaving us the lucky ones who can simply walk in their shadows.

Trevaunance Cove, St Agnes. A reef of granite blocks is all that remains of the several attempts to create a harbour here.